PRIMARY SOURCE
EXPLORERS

A JOURNEY WITH JUAN PONCE DE LEÓN

LAURA HAMILTON WAXMAN

LERNER PUBLICATIONS ◆ MINNEAPOLIS

To Debra,
my fellow voyager through life

Content consultant:
Sarah Chambers, PhD, History, University of Wisconsin, Madison
Professor in the Department of History, University of Minnesota

Lerner Publications Company
A division of Lerner Publishing Group, Inc.
241 First Avenue North
Minneapolis, MN USA 55401

For reading levels and more information, look up this title at www.lernerbooks.com.

Main body text set in AvenirLTPro 12/18.
Typeface provided by Linotype AG.

Library of Congress Cataloging-in-Publication Data

Names: Waxman, Laura Hamilton, author.
Title: A journey with Juan Ponce de Leon / Laura Hamilton Waxman.
Description: Minneapolis : Lerner Publications, 2017. | Series: Primary
    source explorers | Includes bibliographical references and index. |
    Audience: Grades 4 to 6. | Audience: Ages 8 to 11.
Identifiers: LCCN 2016010666 (print) | LCCN 2016014173 (ebook) | ISBN
    9781512407761 (lb : alk. paper) | ISBN 9781512410990 (eb pdf)
Subjects: LCSH: Ponce de Leon, Juan, 1460?–1521—Juvenile literature.
    | Explorers—America—Biography—Juvenile literature. | Explorers—
    Spain—Biography—Juvenile literature. | Florida—Discovery and
    exploration—Spanish—Juvenile literature. | America—Discovery and
    exploration—Spanish—Juvenile literature.
Classification: LCC E125.P7 W39 2017 (print) | LCC E125.P7 (ebook) | DDC
    910.92—dc23

LC record available at http://lccn.loc.gov/2016010666

Manufactured in the United States of America
1-39348-21160-10/31/2016

CONTENTS

 = Denotes primary source

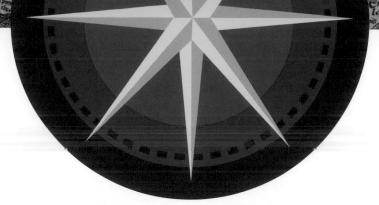

INTRODUCTION
OPENING THE DOOR
TO THE PAST

Juan Ponce de León lived in a time long before videos, photographs, and social media recorded the details of people's lives. Yet historians have been able to piece together the basic facts of this explorer's life. How do they do it? They carefully examine primary sources.

Primary sources are written documents, images, and other objects created when a historical person lived. Some of the richest primary sources are diaries, letters, and government records. Primary sources can also be maps, artwork, tools, and other artifacts.

This letter from Spanish royalty was delivered to Ponce de León in 1493. Letters written during Ponce de León's lifetime are extremely valuable primary sources for historians who work to piece together details about the explorer's life.

Artwork can be an especially fascinating primary source. This portrait of Ponce de León was created in 1513 and gives us a good idea of what he looked like then.

Together, they provide a firsthand account of what life was like in the past. They help to paint a picture of the thoughts, motivations, and experiences of a person who lived long ago.

If Ponce de León kept a journal or a ship's log, is has not survived. But other primary sources do exist that open the door to his adventurous life. These include the writings of historians living in his era, several letters of Ponce de León's, and images from his time. As you learn about Ponce de León's explorations, you'll be able to read or examine some of those primary sources for yourself.

CHAPTER 1
AN EXPLORER IS BORN

This work of art depicting Ponce de León was not created during the explorer's lifetime, so it is not a primary source.

Juan Ponce de León was likely born around 1474. He grew up in Santervás de Campos, a village in northwestern Spain. His father was a wealthy Spanish nobleman, but historians believe Ponce de León's father may not have been married to his mother. Ponce de León grew up knowing he would inherit little, if anything, from his father. Somehow, he would have to make his own way in the world.

By the age of ten, Ponce de León was working as an assistant to a Spanish knight. At the time, the Spanish kingdom of Castile was involved in an ongoing war against Muslim kingdoms in southern Spain. Young Ponce de León received some training in combat and experienced battle firsthand. In 1492 the warring ended in Spanish victory. Suddenly, he was out of a job. Luckily for him, a new adventure at sea awaited.

THE AGE OF EXPLORATION

That year Italian explorer Christopher Columbus discovered what Europeans came to call the New World. Of course, this land on the other side of the globe wasn't new at all. Indigenous peoples had discovered North and South America long before. They had been living and thriving there for thousands of years. But these continents, full of valuable natural resources, were new to Europeans. And Europeans were hungry to explore and claim this New World for themselves.

Mapping was in its early days when Ponce de León was young. This map, created in the late fifteenth century, shows the world as people thought it looked at that time.

This portrait of Christopher Columbus was created in the nineteenth century, long after both Columbus and Ponce de León lived.

The king and queen of Spain had paid for Columbus's first voyage to the New World. They hoped to increase their country's wealth and power. When Columbus returned to Spain, he told them of the great riches to be found in the land he'd journeyed to, especially gold. Word of Columbus's success spread. It excited people's imaginations and inspired a new age of exploration among Europeans.

The timing couldn't have been better for Ponce de León. The young man was penniless and searching for a new way to support himself. He set his sights on life as an explorer.

WHAT DO YOU THINK?

Each time Europeans set sail for an unknown land in the New World, they were risking their lives. Why do you think the Spanish people treated a voyage to the New World as a cause for celebration? What do you think they expected would happen on these voyages?

SETTING SAIL

It's believed that Ponce de León joined Columbus on his second voyage in September 1493. He was aboard one of seventeen Spanish ships prepared to set sail for the Caribbean from Cádiz, Spain. A passenger named Guglielmo Coma wrote a letter about this experience. He said that a crowd gathered to see the ships off while the crew came together in prayer for a safe voyage. It was a moment of celebration and excitement:

> The ships were hung with banners; streamers were flying from the rigging; . . . The shores echoed the blare of trumpets and the blasting of horns, and even the sea bottom echoed the cannons' roar.

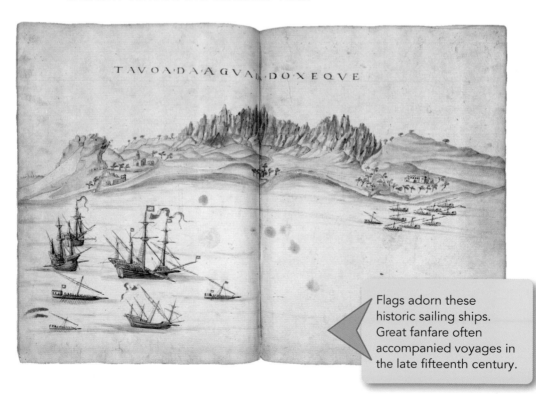

Flags adorn these historic sailing ships. Great fanfare often accompanied voyages in the late fifteenth century.

For Ponce de León, it was his first voyage at sea. He had to adjust to life on a ship, and it wouldn't be easy. A Spanish traveler on a similar voyage to the Caribbean eighty years later described his experiences in painful detail. According to Eugenio de Salazar, "The force of the sea did such violence to our stomachs that . . . [we were] spewing from our mouths all that had entered therein that day."

Salazar also compared his ship to a stinking city. He wrote that it was full of people, lice, cockroaches, and rats. He described the filthy drinking water and bad food. But he also wrote about the hardworking sailors. And he described the joy everyone felt when they at last sighted land.

The three ships Columbus took on his first voyage to the New World appear in this painting from the nineteenth century.

This painting from the 1490s shows ships called naos as they looked when Ponce de León joined Columbus on his second voyage in 1493.

SPANISH SHIPS

Spanish explorers in Ponce de León's time relied on two types of ships. Naos, or carracks, were heavy-duty ships. They had deep hulls (frames made up of a ship's deck, sides, and bottom) that could carry up to 2,000 tons (1,814 metric tons) of cargo. Caravels were lighter, faster ships. They were also easier to maneuver in tight spaces. What both ships had in common was their dependence on wind. Without wind filling their sails, they wouldn't get very far.

SAFE LANDING

Columbus's fleet of ships reached land in November 1493. They then headed for the Caribbean island of Hispaniola. Along the way, Columbus sighted and claimed a number of Caribbean islands. These included modern-day Montserrat, Antigua, Saint Croix, and Puerto Rico.

In Hispaniola, Ponce de León would have learned about the extreme dangers of setting up a new colony firsthand. Columbus had left behind nearly forty Spanish men on that island in hopes of establishing a Spanish colony. Upon his return, he discovered that all of them were dead. Disease had killed some. The others had died at the hands of the Taino people who had settled the island hundreds of years earlier.

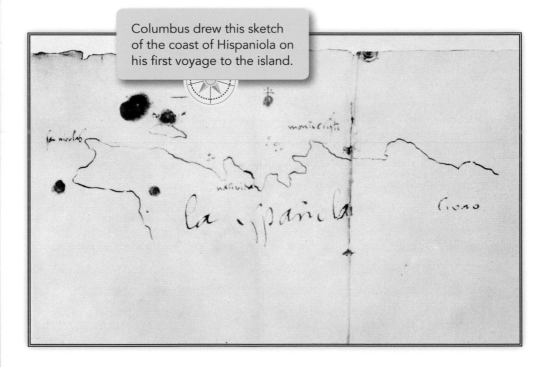

Columbus drew this sketch of the coast of Hispaniola on his first voyage to the island.

The Taino had a well-established culture and society long before Europeans arrived in their home. This nineteenth-century engraving, created many years after Ponce de León lived, depicts a Taino village.

Columbus was determined to maintain Spain's claim on the island. He quickly established another colony in modern-day Dominican Republic. Ponce de León may have been one of the first Europeans to set foot in this new settlement. He may have even stayed there and lived among the Taino, learning their language and way of life. More likely, he simply sailed back to Spain with Columbus. Either way, he'd gotten a taste of life as a Spanish explorer, and he was ready for more.

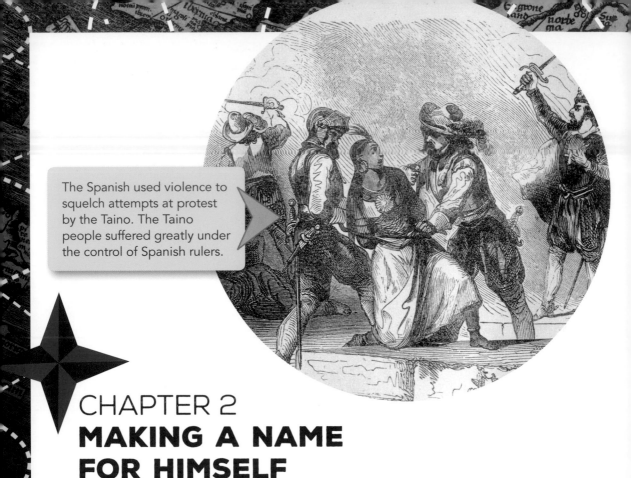

The Spanish used violence to squelch attempts at protest by the Taino. The Taino people suffered greatly under the control of Spanish rulers.

CHAPTER 2
MAKING A NAME FOR HIMSELF

No one knows for certain what Ponce de León did between 1494 and 1501. No reliable primary sources mention him or his whereabouts during those years. What is known is that he was in Hispaniola in 1502, in a Spanish settlement called Santo Domingo. It's possible he sailed there from Spain with Nicolás de Ovando. Spain's king and queen had sent Ovando to Santo Domingo to govern the struggling colony.

VIOLENCE BREAKS OUT

The Taino on the island had suffered terribly under Spanish rule. The Spanish newcomers had unknowingly spread

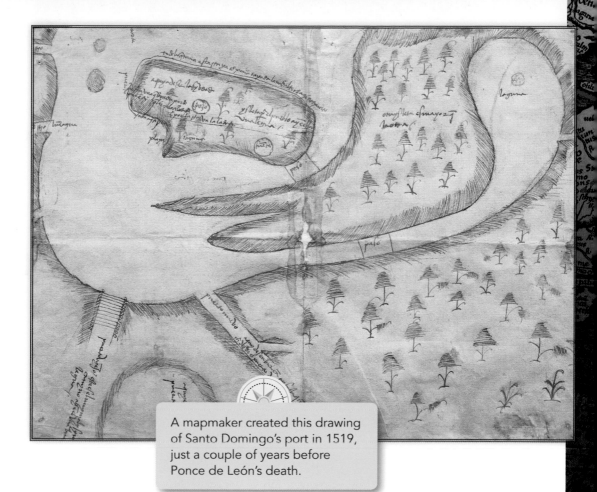

A mapmaker created this drawing of Santo Domingo's port in 1519, just a couple of years before Ponce de León's death.

measles and smallpox. These European diseases killed many of the Taino. The Spanish had also forced hundreds of Taino to mine for gold under harsh conditions. In exchange, they promised food, housing, protection, and wages. But the Spanish colonists rarely kept their promises. The frustrated Taino threatened to rebel. Governor Ovando's new job was to maintain strict control over them and keep them working. He was also expected to increase the amount of gold mined on the island. That way, more gold could be sent back to Spain.

Controlling rebelling Taino often meant killing them, which Ovando ordered his men to do. The Taino fought back by attacking and burning a Spanish fort. Then Ovando ordered about four hundred Spaniards to stage a counterattack. One of the leaders of this attack was Ponce de León. His early years in the military gave him a major advantage. Even though he and his men were outnumbered four to one, they defeated the Taino.

Ponce de León's success impressed Ovando. The governor granted him many acres of land in eastern Hispaniola. He also gave Ponce de León some Taino slaves to work his land. Even more important, Ovando put Ponce de León in charge

An undated work of art shows the conflict on Hispaniola between Europeans and the Taino.

Growing two simple crops—sweet potatoes and cassava—helped Ponce de León come into tremendous personal wealth.

of the eastern half of Hispaniola. His job was to increase gold mining and maintain Spain's claim on the land. Ponce de León also had to provide Spanish colonists with farmland and Taino workers.

WEALTHY LANDOWNER

Almost overnight, Ponce de León transitioned from a man of very modest means to a landowner with plenty of wealth and power. Relying on the labor of enslaved Taino, Ponce de León mined the area for gold. He sent much of it back to the king and queen in Spain. For himself, Ponce de León raised horses, pigs, and cattle. He also grew cassava and sweet potatoes. He made his fortune by selling crops, cassava bread, and livestock to ships stopping in a nearby bay to load up on supplies.

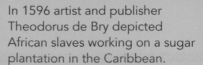
In 1596 artist and publisher Theodorus de Bry depicted African slaves working on a sugar plantation in the Caribbean.

SLAVERY IN THE CARIBBEAN

The Spanish colonists on Hispaniola often treated the Taino as slaves. As the colony grew, the Spanish needed more labor to farm the land and mine for gold. In 1502 they began kidnapping and bringing African slaves to the island. Europeans in the Caribbean came to rely more heavily on African slaves. Because of this, the black population on the island became very large.

A NEW SPANISH SETTLEMENT

In 1505 Ponce de León established a new Spanish town in eastern Hispaniola. He named it Salvaleón and built a huge stone house for himself and his young family. He had fallen in love with and married a Spanish woman named Leonora. Her father ran an inn in Santo Domingo. Together, the couple would have three daughters and a son.

Life was going well for Ponce de León. But his adventurous spirit made him restless. He wanted to explore more lands for Spain, send back more gold, and bring more honor to himself.

WHAT DO YOU THINK?

Do you think Ponce de León should have accepted land and Taino laborers as a reward for his military victory in Hispaniola? What do these actions tell you about his attitude toward indigenous peoples?

This oil painting shows King Ferdinand around the year 1500. The Spanish king was eager to colonize the Caribbean.

CHAPTER 3
IN SEARCH OF GOLD

Ponce de León had heard rumors from Taino people of gold to be found on another nearby island. Columbus had named this island San Juan Bautista. Later, it became known as Puerto Rico, which means "rich port" in Spanish. After discussing things with Ovando, Ponce de León received permission to explore and colonize that island. His goal was to seek more farmland for the Spanish colonists and mine for as much gold as possible. This plan pleased Spain's King Ferdinand, who wanted Spanish control over Puerto Rico.

NEW SETTLEMENT, MORE WEALTH
Sometime between 1506 and 1508, Ponce de León established

a Spanish capital in Puerto Rico. He named it Caparra. It was on a hill in the middle of a swamp, which made it hard to invade. That would have been important for Ponce de León and the other Spanish colonists living there. The island was home to both the Taino and their powerful enemy, the Caribs. The Caribs were indigenous people known for their fierce fighting skills. Ponce de León promised to protect the Taino from the Caribs. In exchange, the Taino agreed to work the land and mine for gold.

The ruins of Ponce de León's stone home in Caparra still exist. Behind them in this photo is a museum built in modern times.

As a reward for his successes, King Ferdinand named Ponce de León governor of Puerto Rico. Ponce de León built another large stone house in Caparra and brought his family to live with him. Meanwhile, he still claimed profits from his farmland on Hispaniola. He was wealthier and more powerful than ever. But with that power came responsibility.

FAIR FOR HIS TIMES

Ponce de León had a reputation for being a good governor who tried to treat the Taino laborers fairly. But that didn't

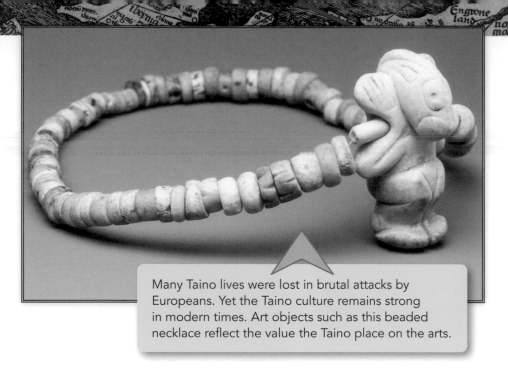

Many Taino lives were lost in brutal attacks by Europeans. Yet the Taino culture remains strong in modern times. Art objects such as this beaded necklace reflect the value the Taino place on the arts.

mean he stopped assigning Taino to work for colonists on the island. Some of those colonists mistreated the Taino. European diseases also weakened the indigenous community. Just as they had on Hispaniola, the Taino eventually fought back by killing many Spanish colonists. Ponce de León knew that his job was to maintain Spain's claim to the valuable land. In 1511 he ordered his men to launch a surprise nighttime attack on the Taino. Thousands of Taino were killed. In this way, his men ruthlessly put down the Taino rebellion.

DIEGO COLUMBUS CAUSES TROUBLE

That same year, trouble came in another form—Christopher Columbus's oldest son, Diego Columbus. The elder Columbus had died in 1506. But his family argued that the land he had claimed for Spain was theirs to govern and profit from. King Ferdinand disagreed. He tried to block this claim, but Diego Columbus fought back.

In 1511 he won the right to be viceroy of the Caribbean islands that his father had discovered. Immediately, he chose a new governor for Puerto Rico and took away most of Ponce de León's power. Ponce de León was also in danger of losing his good reputation. Because Ponce de León remained loyal to the king, Columbus had his men spread nasty rumors about him.

Ponce de León had made a good life for himself in Puerto Rico, but that life had been taken away. Perhaps it was time for another adventure.

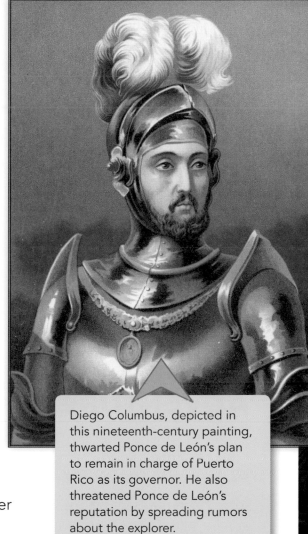

Diego Columbus, depicted in this nineteenth-century painting, thwarted Ponce de León's plan to remain in charge of Puerto Rico as its governor. He also threatened Ponce de León's reputation by spreading rumors about the explorer.

WHAT DO YOU THINK?

In Ponce de León's time, expanding Spain's claim to land, power, and gold in the New World was a path to great honor among Europeans. Can you think of similar accomplishments or goals that we honor in modern times? Do you agree or disagree with the importance of these achievements?

The Bahamas, which King Ferdinand wanted Ponce de León to explore, is extremely rich with plants and wildlife.

CHAPTER 4
A RISKY ADVENTURE

King Ferdinand hadn't forgotten about Ponce de León. He began encouraging the explorer to sail north to Bimini. This island is in the Bahamas, a large cluster of islands in the Caribbean. Ferdinand hoped that Ponce de León would find lots of gold and fertile farmland there.

TAKING A GAMBLE

The king drew up a contract for the voyage. In part, it said, "You may go to discover [Bimini] with ships you wish to take at your own cost. . . . When you find and discover [the] island, you shall be obliged to settle [it] at your own cost." So Ponce de León

This map, created around 1500 by navigator Juan de la Cosa, shows Bimini and other areas that de la Cosa saw in his travels.

would have to pay for this entire adventure with his own money. That was a huge risk. If he failed to find and settle Bimini, he would lose a fortune.

But if Ponce de León was successful, he would profit greatly. The king's contract promised Ponce de León much of "the gold, and other metals and profitable things" found on Bimini in the first ten years. The king also promised to grant Ponce de León "the government and justice of [Bimini] for all the days of your life." That meant Ponce de León would be in charge of the island until he died. Best of all, he would gain the glory that came with expanding Spain's empire.

He decided to take the king up on his offer. For the next eleven months, Ponce de León gathered food and supplies for his voyage. He also put together a crew for three small ships, the *Santiago*, the *Santa María de la Consolación*, and the *San Cristóbal*.

This undated illustration shows Ponce de León receiving water from the mythical Fountain of Youth.

THE FOUNTAIN OF YOUTH

Legend has it that the true reason for Ponce de León's voyage was to find the Fountain of Youth. This source of natural spring water was supposed to make people young again. The legend about Ponce de León comes from a primary source. It was written by Spanish historian Gonzalo Fernández de Oviedo y Valdés in the sixteenth century. Oviedo wrote that Ponce de León was sent to Bimini to find these magical waters.

But not all primary sources are reliable. Many historians think Oviedo made up this story. Others believe that Ponce de León may have kept an eye out for the Fountain of Youth. But his main goal was finding valuable farmland and gold.

SAILING TO FLORIDA

Ponce de León's small fleet set sail on the evening of March 4, 1513. With him were about sixty-five people, including some Taino and Africans to work the land. A month later, the ships reached a large, unknown island. Ponce de León called it La Florida. He didn't realize that Florida was actually a peninsula attached to the North American continent.

Ponce de León is often remembered as being the first European to discover Florida. In truth, a few other Europeans had already been there. They had stayed just long enough to kidnap American Indians for the slave trade. But Ponce de León was the first European to arrive in Florida with the goal of starting a permanent settlement there.

This sailing ship was designed to replicate the ships that Ponce de León used to sail to Bimini.

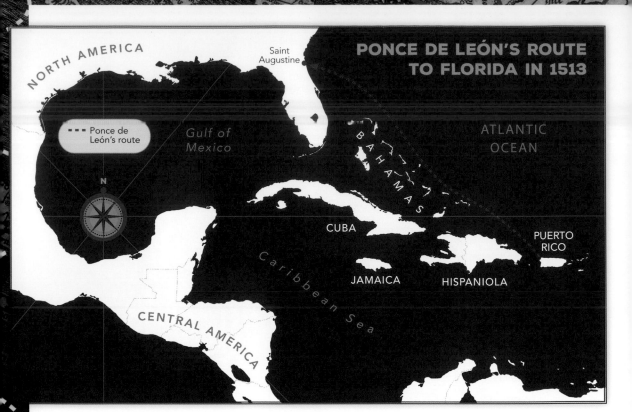

NORTH AMERICA

Saint
Augustine

- - - Ponce de
León's route

Gulf of
Mexico

ATLANTIC
OCEAN

B A H A M A S

N

CUBA

PUERTO
RICO

Caribbean Sea

JAMAICA

HISPANIOLA

CENTRAL AMERICA

UNFRIENDLY ENCOUNTERS

The American Indians living in Florida included the Timucua,
Tequesta, and Calusa peoples. Their experiences with
Europeans had been negative, and they distrusted Ponce de
León and his men from the start. In 1601 a Spanish historian
named Antonio de Herrera y Tordesillas described an early
encounter between them and Ponce de Leon's men:

> The Indians, with their arrows and spears, with points
> made from sharpened bone of fish spines, wounded
> two [Spanish men]. . . . Juan Ponce collected his
> men, with some difficulty, and they departed during
> the night.

Historian Antonio de Herrera y Tordesillas, who wrote the only primary-source account of Ponce de León's time in Florida

Herrera's history is the only primary source that gives details about Ponce de León's 230 days in Florida. According to this historian, Ponce de León had several other conflicts with American Indians. So he decided to leave Florida without establishing a settlement. Besides, he'd found no signs of gold.

WHAT DO YOU THINK?

Are you surprised that Ponce de León agreed to sail to Florida and try to settle it at his own expense? Why do you think the king set up the contract this way? How much faith do you think he had in Ponce de León?

capitan General, año de 1525.

Hernán Cortés appears in fine armor in this 1525 painting created by an artist who lived at the same time as the explorer.

CHAPTER 5
THE FINAL VOYAGE

Ponce de León returned home to more bad news. Carib people had burned Caparra and his house to the ground. His wife and children had barely escaped with their lives. Despite these setbacks, he still hoped to achieve fame and fortune. He agreed to go on a second voyage to explore Florida.

A NEW COMPETITOR

Before Ponce de León could begin this voyage, King Ferdinand died. Ponce de León soon returned to Spain. He needed to gain favor with Ferdinand's grandson, King Carlos I. To keep his power and wealth, Ponce de León had to prove his worth to this new king.

In 1519 Ponce heard about a skilled but ruthless Spanish explorer named Hernán Cortés. Cortés was making a name for himself. He had been forming alliances with indigenous groups in Mexico to seize control of the wealthy Aztec Empire. Ponce de León worried that Cortés or someone else might try to settle nearby Florida too. He also worried that Cortés would outshine him in the eyes of King Carlos. Ponce de León prepared for his second voyage to Florida.

This eighteenth-century engraving shows Ponce de León in his later years, around the time the explorer embarked on his second voyage to Florida.

SETTING SAIL ONCE AGAIN

By early 1521, Ponce de León had two ships, supplies, and a crew. But few primary sources exist about his second voyage to Florida. For example, no one recorded the names of the ships Ponce de León and his men departed in on February 20. Most of the one hundred to two hundred people on board have also been forgotten. It's not even known exactly when Ponce de León and his crew reached Florida's shores.

FAILURE IN FLORIDA

Ponce de León's attempts to claim Florida did not go as planned. In July 1521, he and his men got caught up in a deadly battle against some Calusa fighters. During the battle, an arrow hit him in the thigh and badly wounded him. He and his men fled Florida. They sailed to a Spanish settlement in nearby Cuba. By then his wound had become infected. The infection spread, and Ponce de León died soon after. He was about forty-seven years old.

DIRECTIONS FROM THE KING

Ponce de León's contract from the king described exactly how he was to treat the American Indians in Florida. His main goal was to make sure that they gave their land over to Spanish control. If they refused, Ponce de León was supposed to

make war and seize them and take them away as slaves. But if they do obey, give them the best treatment possible and try, as it is stated, by every means at your disposal to convert them to our Holy Catholic Faith.

This quote shows that a second goal of Spain was to spread Christianity to the New World.

A LASTING IMPACT

Ponce de León's last risky adventure did not pay off for Spain right away. But his landing on Florida inspired others to return and start new settlements. The first of those settlements was Saint Augustine, the oldest city in the United States.

Ponce de León spent his life seeking new lands in the New World. His adventurous spirit, loyalty to his kingdom, and willingness to take risks helped him make history.

The founding of Saint Augustine, Florida, is shown in this work of art. Saint Augustine remains rich with history in modern times.

WHAT DO YOU THINK?

Based on the primary sources about Ponce de León and his times, what is your view of him? Do you agree that he's an important historical figure? Do you think he was honorable? Why or why not?

TIMELINE

1474 Juan Ponce de León is born around this time in Santervás de Campos, Spain.

1493 Ponce de León likely sails with Christopher Columbus on his second voyage to the New World.

1504 Ponce de León helps to defeat a Taino rebellion in Hispaniola. As a reward, he receives land and leadership duties on the eastern part of the island.

1505 He establishes a new settlement on Hispaniola, which he names Salvaleón.

1506 He makes his first voyage to Puerto Rico and may have begun to establish Caparra.

1509 King Ferdinand appoints Ponce de León governor of Puerto Rico.

1511 Ponce de León orders his men to kill thousands of Taino in Puerto Rico to stop their rebellion. In May, Diego Columbus replaces Ponce de León with a different governor.

1512 Ponce de León agrees to a contract with King Ferdinand to voyage to the island of Bimini at his own expense.

1513 Ponce de León sets sail for Bimini on March 4 but ends up anchoring at Florida in April.

1514 He agrees to another royal contract for a second voyage to Florida.

1516 King Ferdinand dies. He is replaced by King Carlos I, his grandson.

1519 Hernán Cortés invades Mexico and discovers gold and wealthy indigenous settlements there.

1521 Ponce de León sets sail for his second voyage to Florida on February 20. In July he is struck by an arrow during a battle with Calusa Indians. He dies in Cuba soon after.

SOURCE NOTES

9   Robert H. Fuson, *Juan Ponce de Leon and the Spanish Discovery of Puerto Rico and Florida* (Blacksburg, VA: McDonald & Woodward, 2000), 34–35.

10   Ibid., 41.

24   Ibid., 92.

25   Ibid., 93.

25   Ibid.

28   Ibid., 106.

32   Ibid., 130.

GLOSSARY

artifact: an object that shows human work and represents a culture

cassava: a plant with roots that are used to make a white starch called tapioca

colony: a foreign territory that is controlled by or belongs to another country

contract: a legal agreement

empire: a political unit with a territory or several territories under one ruler who has total control

fleet: a group of ships that move or work together

indigenous: originally from a particular place. Indigenous peoples are native to that area.

peninsula: a piece of land that is surrounded almost entirely by water and is attached to a larger land

viceroy: a person sent by a king or queen to rule a colony

SELECTED BIBLIOGRAPHY

Allman, T. D. *Finding Florida: The True History of the Sunshine State.* New York: Atlantic Monthly, 2013.

Fuson, Robert H. *Juan Ponce de Leon and the Spanish Discovery of Puerto Rico and Florida.* Blacksburg, VA: McDonald & Woodward, 2000.

Schultz, Colin. "Setting Sail: The 500th Anniversary of Juan Ponce de León's Discovery of Florida." *Smithsonian.com*, March 27, 2013. http://www.smithsonianmag.com/smart-news/setting-sail-the -500th-anniversary-of-juan-ponce-de-leons-discovery-of-florida -10197205/?no-ist.

Shaer, Matthew. "Ponce de Leon Never Searched for the Fountain of Youth." *Smithsonian Magazine*, June 2013. http://www .smithsonianmag.com/history/ponce-de-leon-never-searched -for-the-fountain-of-youth-72629888/?no-ist.

Turner, Samuel P. "The Caribbean World of Juan Ponce de León and His Discovery of Florida." Culturally La Florida. Accessed December 20, 2015. http://www.culturallylaflorida.org/papers /Turner_CaribbeanWorld.pdf.

FURTHER INFORMATION

The Age of Discovery
http://exploration.marinersmuseum.org/type/age-of-discovery
Learn about the explorers, ships, and tools of Ponce de León's era in history.

History: Ponce de León
http://www.history.com/topics/exploration/juan-ponce-de-leon
Visit this web page about Ponce de León and read a brief biography about him and his journeys. You'll also find a video about whether the Fountain of Youth exists.

Kallen, Stuart A. *A Journey with Christopher Columbus.* Minneapolis: Lerner Publications, 2018. Read about the man who gave Ponce de León his first opportunity to go on an ocean voyage.

Owens, Lisa L. *A Journey with Hernán Cortés.* Minneapolis: Lerner Publications, 2018. Learn more about one of Ponce de León's fellow explorers and competitors.

Sammons, Sandra Wallus. *Ponce de León and the Discovery of Florida.* Sarasota, FL: Pineapple Press, 2013. Learn more about this Spanish explorer.

Expand learning beyond the printed book. Download free, complementary educational resources for this book from our website, www.lerneresource.com.

INDEX

PHOTO ACKNOWLEDGMENTS

The images in this book are used with the permission of: Library of Congress, map background; © Album/Oronoz/SuperStock, p. 4; © DEA/G. DAGLI ORTI/Getty Images, p. 5; © Stock Montage/Archive Photos/Getty Images, p. 6; © Roger Viollet/Getty Images, p. 7; © Monastery of La Rabida, Huelva, Andalusia, Spain/Bridgeman Images, p. 8; © Wikimedia Commons, p. 9; © Private Collection/Index/Bridgeman Images, p. 10; © INTERFOTO/Alamy, p. 11; © Private Collection/Bridgeman Images, p. 12; © De Agostini Picture Library/G. Dagli Orti/Bridgeman Images, p. 13; Iberfoto/Courtesy Everett Collection, p. 14; © DeAgostini/SuperStock, p. 15; © Everett Historical/Shutterstock.com, p. 16; © FLO/Science and Society/SuperStock, p. 17; The Granger Collection, New York, pp. 18, 25, 31; © Musee Sainte-Croix, Poitiers, France/Bridgeman Images, p. 20; Laura Magruder/El Nuevo Dia de Puerto Rico/Newscom, p. 21; © Dirk Bakker/Museo del Hombre Dominicano, Dominican Republic/Bridgeman Images, p. 22; © Private Collection/Look and Learn/Bridgeman Images, p. 23; © iStockphoto.com/erikruthoff, p. 24; © Bettmann/Getty Images, p. 26; Andrew Innerarity/REUTERS/Newscom, p. 27; © Laura Westlund/Independent Picture Service, p. 28; © Universal History Archive/Getty Images, p. 29; © Museo de la Ciudad, Mexico/Index/Bridgeman Images, p. 30; © Private Collection/Peter Newark American Pictures/Bridgeman Images, p. 33.

Cover: © Lanmas/Alamy (portrait); Library of Congress (map background).